Transformed
Living in
Tough Times

ALSO BY JOHN ED MATHISON

Transformed Giving

Treasures of the Transformed Life

Extra Effort

Fishing for Birds

Every Member in Ministry

Transformed Living in Tough Times

JOHN ED MATHISON

Abingdon Press / Nashville

TRANSFORMED LIVING IN TOUGH TIMES

Copyright © 2009 by Abingdon Press

All rights reserved.

This book is printed on acid-free, elemental-chlorine–free paper.

CIP data has been applied for.

ISBN: 978-0-687-65707-0

09 10 11 12 13 14 15 16 17 18 — 10 9 8 7 6 5 4 3 2 1

MANUFACTURED IN THE UNITED STATES OF AMERICA

Contents

"I tell you not to worry about everyday life—whether you have enough food and drink, or enough clothes to wear. Isn't life more than food, and your body more than clothing? Look at the birds. They don't plant or harvest or store food in barns, for your heavenly Father feeds them. And aren't you far more valuable to him than they are? Can all your worries add a single moment to your life?

"And why worry about your clothing? Look at the lilies of the field and how they grow. They don't work or make their clothing, yet Solomon in all his glory was not dressed as beautifully as they are. And if God cares so wonderfully for wildflowers that are here today and thrown into the fire tomorrow, he will certainly care for you. Why do you have so little faith?

"So don't worry about these things, saying, 'What will we eat? What will we drink? What will we wear?' These things dominate the thoughts of unbelievers, but your heavenly Father already knows all your needs. Seek the Kingdom of God above all else, and live righteously, and he will give you everything you need."

Matthew 6:25-33 NLT

Introduction

A man and his wife were busily boarding up the windows on their house to withstand the approaching hurricane. As they worked, they noticed an eagle flying high into the sky, several starlings and finches going about their business as though it were just another day, and a rooster racing around the yard crowing frantically. Soon the wind increased; the eagle was flying high above the storm; the starlings and finches were perched on a power line watching the storm move in; and the rooster had folded his wings over his head, rolled over, and played dead. Each, in its own way, was reacting to the tough times ahead.

- On a single day in January 2008, some 70,000 people were laid off, and another 50,000 or 60,000 lost their jobs on each of the ten days that followed.
- Every year 15,000 children are diagnosed with type 1 diabetes. Each year about 1.1 million Americans suffer a heart attack.
- More than 43 percent of first marriages end in separation or divorce within 15 years.

- About 43 percent of the U.S. adult population (76 million people) experienced alcoholism in the family while growing up. Approximately one in five adult Americans (18 percent) lived with an alcoholic while growing up.
- In 2005, Hurricane Katrina killed more than 1,600 people, destroyed 200,000 Gulf Coast homes, and displaced about 1 million people.

When we experience factors beyond our control, whether they are financial, health-related, family-oriented, or the effects of natural disasters, we tend to feel that we can do little to change the situation. We develop feelings of helplessness, anger, and depression.

Fear of tough times can paralyze the best of us, but it need not be that way for transformed people. God has promised that he will not allow anything to touch his children that has not first passed through his hands. He also promises that we will not be tested beyond our ability to respond.

The fact is, we can rise above the storm during tough times by keeping our focus on God.

Weathering the Storm

We do not have to struggle alone.

God is always with us, in good times and in tough times. We are so precious to God that he has promised to be with us, no matter what we go through.

Jesus has many names in the Bible. One—Immanuel—means "he is with us." In Isaiah 7, the prophet declares that a "virgin will conceive a child! She will give birth to a son and will call him Immanuel (which means 'God is with us')." This verse from Isaiah is repeated in Matthew 1:23.

Then again, Jesus himself declares in Matthew 28:20, "Be sure of this: I am with you always, even to the end of the age" (NLT).

We can share our fears and concerns with God.

Actually, we can, and should, share everything with God, things that we can't share with anyone else. Since he knows it all anyway and knows the end from the beginning, it's not like we're going to surprise him. God knows what we need before we ask (Matthew 6:8).

Do you wonder, then, why we should talk to God, share our heart and our concerns, when he already knows everything anyway? The thing is, every time we pray, we deepen our relationship with the Heavenly Father. Every time we pray we open the door just a little more for God to go deeper into our life, our heart, our thoughts, and our actions.

Prayer allows us to experience God's love and concern for us. When we pray, we discover just how much God loves us and how much he cares. We read in 1 James 1:5 "If you need wisdom, ask our generous God, and he will give it to you. He will not rebuke you for asking" (NLT).

We can team with other Christians.

When we surround ourselves with other Christians and remind one another that we're all in this together, we can accomplish so much more. We are more willing to step out and take risks when we know that we're not alone. Teaming with other Christians gives us moral support, keeps us on target when we get frustrated, and encourages us to go for it even during tough times. In Galatians 6:2, Paul says, "Share each other's burdens, and in this way obey the law of Christ" (NLT).

The Purpose of This Book

All of us experience rainy days and sunshiny days—scale mountains and navigate the valleys—enjoy good days and trudge through tough times. People who live in tough times become either bitter or better. Tough times either make or break a person. However, transformed people face tough times in a unique way. We have resources that help us choose the right path.

Consider a rooster's reaction to a coming storm. I have been told that when a storm blows in, a rooster will get all excited, running around the yard, cackling, and creating chaos among the hens. He actually causes a storm in his immediate environment that might be as big as the one that is developing from the weather. I understand that his final act of chaos is to flap his wings over his head, fall down, and play dead.

Transformed people react more like the eagle that faces a storm in a totally different way. Rather than running around and creating chaos, an eagle simply lifts his wings and allows the wind of the approaching storm to lift him high, above the danger.

Tough times don't destroy transformed people. Tough times lift us to a new level of faith and living.

Part of a bird's success in weathering a storm is its ability to sense when the storm is coming. As the apostle Paul referred to the necessity of a "wake-up call" (Romans 13:11), we too need to wake up to the tough things that are happening around us. Tough times are a wake-up call for transformed people—an alarm clock that gets our attention and propels us higher and closer to God.

In this study we will learn how transformed living can help us, as people of faith, rise above the storm. We will discover some ways to gauge tough times and learn to handle them effectively. We will look at four practical elements of navigating tough times. Transformed people

1. Return to priorities
2. Focus on fundamentals
3. Exercise God's creativity
4. Develop a Christlike attitude

1.
Return to Priorities

*B*irds are sometimes picked up by strong wind currents and carried long distances. Many new sightings of unusual birds occur after particularly difficult storms. As the birds adapt to their new location, volunteer birders go out to search for and count the number of new birds found in the area.

We all experience tough times—financial problems, health-related challenges, family issues, and the effects of natural disasters. We can allow these issues to engulf us and leave us feeling helpless, angered, and depressed. Or, as transformed people, we can turn our focus to God and rise above the tough times.

Transformed people know the importance of returning to priorities.

Losing Our Way

It is easy to allow our priorities to become inverted. It is not intentional, but a lack of focus causes us to drift.

The Bible teaches us that we are like sheep—we stray from

our points of security. Sheep don't wake up in the morning and say to themselves, "Let's see if we can get lost today." They just wander away from the flock.

I understand a sheep can see only about eight feet away. It looks for a clump of grass and sees one ahead. It wanders over to that clump of grass, and then sees another clump several feet away. It then sees another clump several more feet away. It just keeps its head down looking for grass. Suddenly, it looks up and doesn't see anything familiar and discovers it is lost. It didn't intend to get lost; it just wandered away.

This is the way most of us get lost. We don't wake up and intentionally try to get lost—we just wander.

Psalm 23 was written in a region of desert territory with little green grass. On my first trip to Israel, I thought our experience with sheep would be staged. I figured our hosts would put us on a bus and carry us out to a place where they hired some people to dress up and look like shepherds. But this wasn't the case.

We saw shepherds all around Jerusalem, and we had to be careful as they led their sheep across the roads. Most of the area in southern Israel is very arid, and good green grass is scarce. It is the responsibility of the shepherd to find green pastures where the sheep can graze each day. The sheep can't find green pastures on their own.

Look at Psalm 23:4—"Your rod and your staff protect and comfort me" (NLT). Today, just as in biblical times, shepherds always carry a staff. Staffs give sheep a sense of security and stability. Because sheep can't see very far, when they look up and see a staff they know their shepherd is nearby, watching over them.

Also the Bible says that the sheep know the shepherd's voice (John 10:4), and when a sheep hears a shepherd talking and sees him with a staff, there is a sense that everything will be OK.

Like the sheep, transformed people who look up and see the Good Shepherd watching over us will feel secure in tough times. We know with the Shepherd's help everything will be OK.

How Much Are We Worth?

The transformed person begins with a clear understanding of his or her worth in God's sight. This worth is not predicated on achievements, career advancement, good deeds, leadership positions, or church involvement. It is based solely on God's grace to accept us as we are, redeem us, and give us a purpose for living.

A person's worth seems to be a continuing debate in major league sports as professionals negotiate contracts and free agents look for the best deals.

Defensive tackle Albert Haynesworth went into the free agent market, and the Washington Redskins thought he was worth a lot. He signed a $100 million contract that included a record $41 million signing bonus.

Outfielder Manny Ramirez signed a two-year, $45 million contract with the Los Angeles Dodgers.

Many other players are "testing the market" to see what they are worth. It doesn't appear that the economy is in a downturn when we see what so many of these players are getting.

At the other end of the spectrum is the story of John Odom. He was a former prospect in the San Francisco Giants' minor league system.

Odom grew up in Roswell, Georgia. He played baseball in high school, and then spent a season at Tallahassee Community College before signing with the Giants. After four inconsistent years with the Giants, he was released in 2008. The Canadian Calgary Vipers picked him up; however, because of a 1999 conviction for aggravated assault, Odom was not allowed to enter Canada, so the Vipers traded him to the Texas Laredo Broncos.

The initial trade called for a cash settlement of $1,000 to the Vipers; however, the Canadian team decided they didn't want to do a cash deal because it would make them look financially unstable.

In the end, Odom was traded for ten baseball bats made by a company called Prairie Sticks—a total of $665 for double-dipped black, 34-inch, model C243 baseball bats.

At first the unusual trade was a media-hyped novelty, and Odom actually enjoyed the publicity. But the fun turned to embarrassment as Odom was saddled with nicknames like "Bat Man" or "Bat Guy" or "Bat Boy." His performance for the Broncos suffered, and after only a short time he quit the team in humiliation. Six months later he was found dead from an overdose of drugs and alcohol.

How much was Odom worth—ten bats? Is a football player or baseball player worth $110 million? How much are you worth?

The transformed person focuses on how much he or she is worth to God, not to the world. We are worth everything to him. We are worth so much that he sent his only Son into the world so that whosoever believes in him should never perish but have everlasting life (John 3:16).

Peter reminds us that the faith we have through Jesus Christ is "more precious than gold that perishes" (1 Peter 1:7 NKJV). He also reminds us that when our lives are truly lived according to God's Spirit, we become a "hidden person of the heart, with the incorruptible and unfading charm of a gentle and peaceful spirit, which...is very precious in the sight of God" (1 Peter 3:4 AMP).

Some scientists have estimated the worth of the chemical components of the human body. The dollar amount is not very much—not even the price of ten bats!

It's far more important to know that God calculates the worth of every person by the fact that he created us, loves us, and sent his Son to save us. Each of us is of inestimable worth in God's sight.

Your worth to God is more than any contract that any athlete will ever sign. God will never trade you for anything—not even a few bats or multimillions of dollars.

Ask God to help you today know your worth and live it out accordingly!

Second Things First

Tough times are not always marked by decreased financial resources. Some tough times come when we have more money than we need. The issue that creates tough times is not the amount of money we have but rather getting our priorities straight.

Sometimes we get our priorities out of order. The consequence of getting second things first in a family or in our finances creates tough times. Take for example the teenager who came to me some time ago. She said, "John Ed, I'm terribly upset. You've known our family for years. When we were young we were in Sunday school and church every Sunday. Our family read the Bible and prayed together. Now we don't.

"My dad started getting promotions and making more money, and the more money he made the more he had to work. Gradually, we didn't have time for family devotions. Then we got a house at the lake, and we didn't have time to go to church like we should.

"Now my dad's having trouble with alcohol." Then the young girl broke down and cried. Wiping the tears, she said, "John Ed, he came home this past week and announced that he's leaving. Is there any way we can go back to the way it used to be before we had all of that money? We were happy, and we loved each other. We were devoted, but money has ruined us."

I wish I could say the story had a happy ending, but it didn't. The father ended up losing his job and his family. You see, when we hold so tightly to money that it becomes the most important thing in our lives, everything else gets out of whack. Matthew 6:3

instructs us to make the kingdom of God our primary concern, and when anything else takes first place it becomes an idol. And you know what the Ten Commandments say about idols. The first lesson of a transformed life is to know what comes first. My dad often said it is difficult to hold a full cup with a steady hand, especially if that cup was filled quickly.

The problems of life occur when we put second things first and first things second. Misaligned priorities create havoc within all areas of our life.

A recent news report told of a retired Air Force colonel who almost lost his life when he forgot what to do first. He had decades of experience as a flight instructor, but when giving a flying lesson one afternoon, he forgot about the first lesson. He didn't check the gas gauge!

Now, there are a lot of important aspects to teaching a student to fly—but the first lesson ought to be to check the gas gauge.

Checking the gas gauge first is very important in many areas today. Before cutting the grass, it is good to know how much gas is in the lawn mower. If you run out of gas, it's not detrimental but it is annoying. When you get in a car, check the gas gauge. If you run out of gas in a car, it probably won't be a life-or-death experience, but it does cause a lot of inconvenience. But when you get in an airplane, running out of gas truly is a matter of life and death, not inconvenience or annoyance.

In the same way, missing some life lessons might be just an inconvenience or annoyance. But missing the number-one life lesson is a matter of life and death—now and forever.

The flight instructor was probably busy and rushing to stay on schedule. Likewise, most of us stay very busy and rush through our days. We have a lot to do. With all of our busyness and rushing around, it's easy to overlook the most important thing—our relationship with God.

The flight instructor and his student ran out of fuel near the end of the 45-minute lesson. Miraculously, the instructor was able to bring the single engine plane to a bumpy but safe landing in a field. In our busy days, we may be able to pull off a safe landing in many areas, but all too often we end up sacrificing the most important thing for merely helpful and beneficial things.

Transformed people regularly check priorities so that we don't give primary attention to secondary priorities. We must constantly look at our life to be sure that our first priority is loving God with everything we have. That is the most important thing; everything else comes second.

The main thing is to keep the main thing the main thing, whether you are talking about flying or living!

Misaligned Priorities

We don't intentionally create tough times—they are often a result of our priorities slowly getting out of kilter.

I've enjoyed officiating at a lot of weddings during my ministry. I have never had a couple stand at the altar of the church on their wedding day and say that their goal was to get divorced. The reason couples get divorced is that one unhealthy decision leads to another and to another, and eventually people grow apart. They didn't intend it to happen, but they strayed.

I have had an opportunity to work with many people who suffered alcohol and drug addiction. But I have never had an alcoholic say to me, "John Ed, when I took my first drink, my goal was to see if I could become an alcoholic." We don't intend for that to happen. We just drift in that direction as one drink becomes two and two becomes three. That is why all of us, like sheep, go astray.

Likewise, tough economic and family times often occur because we have allowed one thing to lead us to another and lead us to another. Whenever we stop exercising the practice of proper priorities, it is easy to get lost.

I saw a cute cartoon the other day that showed two sheep that were obviously lost. One sheep said to the other, "We are like humans; we all go astray."

Making Conscious Decisions

In Luke 15:1-7 we read a beautiful story about a shepherd who leaves ninety-nine sheep to go out and look for the one sheep that is lost. When he finds the sheep, he puts it up on his shoulder and brings that sheep back to the fold. He is so happy that he calls his friends to come and rejoice with him.

We need to return to the priority that God is the Good Shepherd who loves his sheep. He finds joy in watching over us and bringing us back to our place of security when we stray.

Transformed people, just like everyone, get bogged down in tough times. However, we can be secure in knowing that the Good Shepherd is passionately searching for those of us who are willing to be found and returned to the fold.

Luke 15:11-32 tells about a man who had two sons. One son thought he had a better financial plan than his dad did. He took his inheritance and went out to execute his plan. It was a disaster. He unintentionally lost everything he was given. He didn't set out to wind up in a pigpen, but he did. Misaligned priorities always lead to a pigpen.

The good news is that the prodigal son "came to his senses" (Luke 15:17). He woke up and began to think rationally. He consciously decided to get up and go home. He gave the pigs a permanent wave! Transformed people consciously decide to leave life's pigpens and go home.

To me, the best part of this story is that the father was already looking for his lost son. Transformed people discover in tough times that when we start looking for God, our Heavenly Father has already decided to search for us. Likewise, in the story we have the beautiful picture of the father receiving the prodigal not as a slave but as a son. He placed a ring on the son's finger and sandals on his feet. He brought out the best food, and a party ensued.

Transformed people enjoy parties in tough times. We experience the love of Abba Father, Daddy God, and his welcome home. We experience the security of the Father's grace.

Transformed people know where security is and allow the Good Shepherd, our Heavenly Father, to carry us there.

Understanding Security

Transformed people understand security. One definition of security is "without anxiety." Too often we think that financial resources provide security. In fact, we refer to stocks and bonds as securities. If you want to see how funny this is, go down to any stock brokerage and watch people gathered around the ticker and see how much "freedom from anxiety" exists there. You don't see much security.

Transformed living is about investing wisely our time, money, talents, and resources. Investments are important. Transformed people understand that God's view of investments is different from the world's view.

In 2008, the world experienced one of the greatest economic revolutions in its history. Who could believe that the stock market would fluctuate 800 points in one day! Who could believe that great companies like AIG, Lehman Brothers, Merrill-Lynch, and Wachovia would ever be in trouble? Who could believe that what happened in the United States could have such a tremendous impact globally, and vice versa?

It is obvious that human theories of economics have been faulty. Maybe it is time that we look at God's economics.

Most folks used to believe that the American economic system was a place where you could put your faith. That belief has been shaken by developments in the stock market and the economy. Many analysts agree that one of the biggest drops in the Dow Jones

Industrial Average during the 1990s was related to the collapse of a big hedge fund called Long-Term Capital Management LP.

This fund was set up by a group of high-powered economists who devised sophisticated models that basically predicted what markets would do and used borrowed money to "hedge." The group included some of the best minds in the economic world. Myron Scholes of MIT and Robert Merton of Harvard both had won Nobel Prizes for economics. David Mullins was the former vice chairman of the Federal Reserve. Their leader was John Meriwether, who pioneered fixed-income arbitrage at Salomon Brothers and built its trading desk into a huge moneymaker.

You would think leadership like that couldn't be wrong. However, it didn't predict what happened in the 1990s, and so it got in trouble. The group made mistakes that required some of America's financial powerhouses to bail them out.

This is just a reminder: God's economics teach that we must invest in eternal things, not worldly things. Even the strongest economic system in the world cannot be completely trusted. Read Matthew 6:19-21 and Matthew 6:25-34. These verses focus on helping us invest our money, time, talents, and energy in things that really matter. Our leader, the Lord Jesus Christ, calls the shots, and he doesn't make any mistakes!

The Bible is our best financial guide!

The Bottom Line

Every business is interested in the bottom line. If a company doesn't show a profit, it doesn't stay around very long. The real focus of human economics is profit.

It is important to know that God understands profit differently. Luke 12 shows us what profit means in God's economics. Jesus told about a man who was a very successful farmer. When the man gathered his crop, his barns were not sufficient to hold it all. So he reasoned, "I know! I'll tear down my barns and build bigger ones. Then I'll have room enough to store all my wheat and other goods. And I'll sit back and say to myself, 'My friend, you have enough stored away for years to come. Now take it easy! Eat, drink, and be merry!'" (Luke 12:18-19 NLT). Notice how many times the pronoun *my* is used.

Human economics viewed the man's profit as an indication that he needed bigger barns. God's economics had a different view. God came to the man and said, "'You fool! You will die this very night. Then who will get everything you worked for?'" (Luke 12:20 NLT). Jesus drove home the message by saying, "Yes, a person is a fool to store up earthly wealth but not have a rich relationship with God" (Luke 12:21 NLT).

Jesus echoed this same thought in Matthew 16:26, when he said, "What profit is it to a man if he gains the whole world, and loses his own soul?" (KJV).

Profit in God's economics is not the accumulation of things; it is the quality of life that results from a relationship with God through Jesus Christ.

In Luke 12, Jesus went on say that we don't have to worry about things to eat, drink, or wear. He said that if we first seek God's Kingdom, then anything we need will be given to us. That is God's economics.

The world's view of profit is summed up in the popular statement, "He who dies with the most toys wins." A lot of people say it and act on it, but it is the opposite of what God's economics teach us.

While human economics are under great scrutiny at this time, and nobody knows where our current economic system will carry us, God's economics have been around for thousands of years and will be here until the end of time!

Our choice is whether to follow human economics or God's economics. Profit is not made up of bottom-line numbers but a top-priority commitment to God's Kingdom.

Transformed people know where real security is—it's in our relationship to our Heavenly Father. The basic priorities are summed up in the question that one young lawyer asked Jesus about inheriting eternal life. Jesus made it very clear that the first priority is to love God with all our heart, mind, and strength. The second priority is to love our neighbors as ourselves. In these two teachings, Jesus stated the most foundational priorities of the Old Testament and New Testament.

Transformed people return to priorities.

2.
Focus on
Fundamentals

Migrating ducks and geese fly in V-shaped formations. They team together and build on one another's strength. Flying in the draft of neighbors' beating wings increases lift and conserves energy. Working together, the ducks and geese can fly a lot farther than one bird trying to make its own way.

The tough times we face in today's troubled world strikes fear even in transformed people. It is then that we must rise above the worldly problems and turn our attentions to the Good Shepherd who is there watching over us. He never forsakes us. He is always with us, even in the darkest hours. He is our guide who leads us safely through the tough times.

The most important thing to remember is that with God, transformed people are never alone. We can take comfort in knowing that we walk with God. We keep our eyes on him, follow in his path, and face the tough times without fear.

Exercise Faith

Transformed people approach tough times not with fear but with faith. In fact, I'm told that the statement that we should not fear appears 365 times in the Bible. I'm not really good with math, but I think that would be about one time for each day— 365 times.

Look at Matthew 14:22-33. Late at night, Jesus startled his disciples, who were in a boat in the middle of a storm-tossed sea. He was walking out on the water to join them when they cried out in fear. Jesus responded, "Don't be afraid.... Take courage. I am here!"

He even allowed Peter to walk on the water. As long as Peter kept his eyes on Jesus, he did what human minds think is impossible and walked on the water. Then, when Peter took his eyes off of Jesus and started looking at the waves and considering the circumstances, he promptly began to sink. Jesus took Peter up out of the water, and Peter resumed walking.

Here's the fundamental principle: if you focus on the circumstances around you every day, you'll be afraid and eventually sink. If you focus on Jesus, you can walk on the water of life. The fundamental is that we are people of faith, not fear.

Focus on the Fundamentals

I have always enjoyed sports. I have competed in basketball, tennis, and racquetball. Through the years, I have learned that successful athletes and coaches focus on the fundamentals.

One of the all-time greatest college football coaches was Paul "Bear" Bryant at the University of Alabama. He is a legend. He was oftentimes quoted as saying, "Don't ever quit doing the things that brung you to the dance." Bryant was a man of fundamentals.

Another great football coach was Vince Lombardi. A story is told about his first team meeting as head coach with the Green Bay Packers. He wanted to make it clear to the players that he was a person who would focus on fundamentals.

To demonstrate the necessity of following all the fundamentals, he reached under his desk, took out a football, and said, "Gentlemen, this is a football."

One of the players, receiver Max McGee, said, "Coach, slow down; you're going a little fast for some of us."

Then there's Bill Walsh, one of the great NFL football coaches. Walsh was the architect of the so-called West Coast offense. He conducted a clinic for NFL quarterbacks. The cost was $10,000 for a week. Most of the NFL teams sent their quarterback to spend the week with Walsh. They believed it would be a good investment.

I was amazed to read that Walsh said to these professional quarterbacks that the biggest problem they faced was to stay focused on the fundamentals. For that reason he spent the first session of the clinic having every quarterback practice taking snaps from the center. Now, these quarterbacks had taken thousands and thousands of snaps since they started playing football. However, Bill Walsh believed if a quarterback couldn't take the snap from the center correctly, the rest of the training would be useless.

It's all about fundamentals. Think about that: professional quarterbacks paying $10,000 to be reminded that they needed to practice taking snaps from the center.

One of the legendary basketball coaches is John Wooden. He had a record of ten national championships at UCLA. From 1971 to 1973, his teams logged eighty-eight consecutive victories! Wooden is a strong Christian gentleman, active in Fellowship of Christian Athletes and an inspiration to all people who love college basketball.

It was said that John Wooden did his recruiting seated at his desk. He didn't have to go out to recruit players; the best players came to him.

Wooden's top priority as a coach was staying focused on the fundamentals. For instance, at his teams' first practice each fall, he would spend the first hour teaching the players how to put on their socks and tie their shoes. His reason for such basic training? If the players didn't put on their socks and shoes correctly, they would get blisters and couldn't carry out the game plan. Just imagine, the best college basketball team in America spending time learning to put on their socks and tie their shoes! These are the fundamentals. It is very important in tough times to focus on fundamentals.

Fear Paralyzes

When San Francisco's Golden Gate Bridge was being built, a lot of folks working on it were afraid of the height. Twenty-three people died as it was being built. Construction was almost stopped because people were so fearful. But then, someone came up with the idea to place a net under the bridge as it was being built to alleviate the workers' fear.

The construction company spent $100,000 for the net, but the plan worked. Knowing that there was a safety net to catch them if they fell, the element of fear was taken from the workers. After the net was installed, there was a 40 percent increase in production from the workers. Only ten people fell after that. It has been said that some of those may have jumped for the fun of it.

Fear paralyzes; faith liberates. Transformed people exercise faith, not fear.

When Jesus invited Peter to step out of the boat and walk on the water, Peter discovered that as long as he trusted Jesus, the water was as solid as a wooden floor. Tough times reveal to us that Jesus is always right. Whenever he invites us to do something different, we can have the confidence that we are able to do it.

Not too long ago, someone shared with me a good definition of fear:

Fear = **F**alse
Evidence
Against
Reality

Transformed people cannot allow false evidence against reality to dominate our lifestyles. The Bible teaches us that God did not give us the sense of fear. Instead, he gave us power, love, and a sound mind (2 Timothy 1:7).

Think about the night that Jesus was born. The Bible tells us that the angels appeared to the shepherds. These normally brave people allowed fear to overtake them. However, the first words of the angel were "Fear not."

Another time, an angel appeared to the women who visited Jesus' tomb on Easter morning. The women were filled with fear and anxiety. Once again, the first words of the angel were "Fear not."

Prime the Pump of Faith

If you swallow the fear, it will poison you. If instead you use it to prime the pump of faith, it will help you rise above the tough times.

Some years ago, near a seldom-used trail in the Amargosa Desert in California, there stood a well that was the only source of water for miles around. Attached to the pump was a tin baking powder can with a message inside, written in pencil on a sheet of brown wrapping paper. The message read:

This pump is all right as of June 1932. I put a new sucker washer into it and it ought to last five years, but the washer dries out and the pump has to be primed. Under the white rock I buried a bottle of water, out of the sun and cork end up. There's enough water to prime this pump, but not if you drink some first. Pour in about a quarter and let her soak to wet the leather. Then pour the rest medium fast and pump like mad. You'll get water. The well never has run dry. Have faith. When you git watered up, fill the bottle and put back like you found it for the next feller.

Signed: Desert Pete

P.S. Don't go drinking the water first! If you do, you won't get no water from the pump, then you'll thirst to death. Prime the pump and you'll get all you can hold.

Desert Pete didn't have a theology degree, but his words remind us of life's basic psychological, physiological, and biblical truths. If you swallow fear, you are doomed. If you use fear to prime the pump of faith, you will have ample resources.

Defining Biblical Faith

It is important to understand what biblical faith is. Many people reject faith because they have expectations of faith that are erroneous. They ask natural questions that come from a secular point of view. Faith doesn't answer those insignificant questions. It answers the big question.

In tough times, we must focus on asking the right questions. We should not spend our time asking why, what, where, or when. Faith does not answer those questions, but it does answer who. Let's look at each of these questions from a biblical point of view.

Faith does not answer the question of why.

"Lord, why is this happening?" "Lord, why me?" It's natural to ask these questions, but faith doesn't answer them. Faith does issue an invitation to trust in God.

Habakkuk, the great prophet, asked why. He said "Lord, why do I look around and see so much wickedness and so much evil? Why is it that evil overcomes or seems to overshadow righteousness?

The whole book of Job focuses on a man who wants to know: "Lord, why is all this happening to me?"

If we knew why, we would know as much as God. And that is humanly impossible. The function of faith is to lead us to trust in

God. Faith won't give us an answer to the question why. The only one who knows why is God himself. What faith says to you and me is that we do not need to know why; we only need to trust.

There were some firefighters out West who went in to fight a fire. There were two brothers in the group. One of the brothers died while fighting the fire and one escaped. The parents of those two boys asked, "Why did one escape and one not escape?"

In south Alabama a beautiful elderly lady had her home flooded for the second time in four years. She asked: "Why did it happen to me? Why did it happen to our little community when it hasn't happened before in a hundred years?"

A young couple got married and boarded an airplane to go to Charlotte, North Carolina, for their honeymoon. That plane crashed. Less than five hours after their wedding, they had died in the plane crash. The paper carried both the announcement of their wedding and the announcement of their death. Their friends asked, "Why did this have to happen?"

Ed Hodge, a Sunday school teacher at Frazer Memorial United Methodist Church in Montgomery, Alabama, was also a pilot. One time he got up at three o'clock in the morning to fly to Tulsa, Oklahoma. The airport was totally dark. He sat in the plane by himself and began to think: "Here I am, trusting a bunch of instruments that I don't understand." As he took off, he listened to a voice coming out of Atlanta. He had never met the person, but he trusted what the person said. Then Ed said it dawned on him: "I can put my trust in a person, and that person may fail me. I can put my trust in airplane instruments, and they may fail me. But when I put my trust in God, he never fails."

The function of faith is not to tell us why something has happened but to lead us to trust. When I can't trace God's hand, I can trust his heart.

Faith does not answer the question of what.

"God, what are you doing?" "God, what's going on in this situation?" "God, what is happening?" These are natural questions, but faith doesn't answer them. Faith does issue an invitation to be obedient and to follow.

In John 13, Jesus took the disciples a basin of water and a rag, then got on his hands and knees and started washing their feet. Immediately Peter said, "Lord, what are you doing?" Jesus said to Peter, "You can't understand that."

God doesn't ask us to understand what is happening; he simply asks us to obey. Jesus said to Peter, "Look, Peter, you don't know what I'm doing, but you just do what I do and serve as I am serving."

Take a look at Acts 3. As Peter and John were walking to the temple to pray, they saw a man who was lame sitting at the gate, begging for money. Peter and John said, "We don't have money but we will give you what we do have. We'll be obedient in the name of Jesus. Rise up and walk." And for the first time, that man's legs received strength, and he jumped up and began running around the community. He ran down to the temple and started praying. Along the way, people asked him, "Man, what is happening to you?" He said, "I don't know—all I did was obey what Peter and John told me to do." The people came to Peter and John and asked in what name—in what power—were they doing this. They said, "It's only in the power of Jesus, and we're simply obeying him."

We don't have to understand what is happening or what is going on. All we need to do is obey, and then God will provide whatever is necessary. We sometimes say, "Lord, what will I do if— What will happen if—" God says, "You don't know the answers to these questions. All I'm asking you to do is simply obey."

God spoke to Noah one day, saying, "Noah, I want you to build an ark." Noah said, "Why in the world would I want to build an ark? God, what are you asking me to do?" God said, "You don't need to know that. Just obey." So Noah started building the ark before it started raining. He just obeyed.

What God desires of you and me is simply to obey him. And once we obey, he will provide whatever is necessary for us as long as we're obedient.

Faith does not answer the question of where.

"Lord, where are you leading me?" "Lord, where is life going?" "Lord, where do you want this church to be?" These are natural questions, but faith doesn't answer them. Faith does issue an invitation to follow God.

Take a look at Genesis 12. In it, God came to Abraham and said, "Abraham, I want you to pick up your tents and your family, and I want you to move out from this land, the Ur of the Chaldees." The first question Abraham asked was, "Lord, where are we going?" The Lord said, "That's not important. All I want you to do is to follow." And so "Abraham followed where God was leading."

In Exodus 3, we read that God came to Moses one day and said, "Moses, I want you to go in and tell Pharaoh to let my people go, and I want you to lead them." And, Moses asked, "Where, Lord?" The Lord said, "Moses, don't ask where. Just follow my directions." You know the rest of the story; Moses took all these people out of Egypt, and he simply followed where God was leading.

Faith is not knowing where you're going. It's trusting and obeying, following wherever God is leading.

One time, the young people at Frazer United Methodist Church returned from camp, having studied the risks of faith. A lot of the young people discovered that the greatest joy in life is to follow Jesus Christ. Some of them committed themselves to full-time Christian service through the church, and we listened intently to what God was doing in their lives. We naturally wanted to ask, "Lord, show us what's down the line for these young people." But God doesn't do that. He says if we have the faith to risk, to take the step, then he'll provide.

One of the best definitions of faith I've ever heard was given to me by one of the young people at Frazer. He passed along something that he had read: "When I walk to the edge of all the light I have and take that step into the darkness of the unknown, I know one of two things will happen. Either there will be solid ground or God will teach me how to fly."

Now that's faith. That's what it means to follow God.

Faith does not answer the question of when.

"Lord, when are you going to do this?" "When is it going to happen?" These are natural questions, but faith doesn't answer them. Faith does issue an invitation to be ready.

In Matthew 24, we read that the disciples asked Jesus, "When are you going to come again?" "When is your Kingdom going to be established?" Jesus replied: "You don't need to know that. Just be ready. Be on the alert. Nobody knows the day or the hour. You just be ready."

Do you know what faith is? Faith is being ready. We don't need to know when. If you want to make money today, write a book predicting when Jesus is coming again and when the world is going to end. More folks will buy that book than you can imagine. In 1988 a man wrote a book titled *88 Reasons Why the Rapture Could Be in 1988*. And, yes, that book sold more than 4 million copies. When the world didn't end in 1988, you know what he did? He simply said that he had made a mistake. Then he wrote the next book, *The Final Shout—Rapture Report 1989*. It sold thousands of copies too.

And you know, right on the front page of the book was a statement saying a person could pay for the book with a Visa charge card and wait a year before actually paying for the book. So, do you think the publisher thought the world was going to end before they got their payment?

Everybody wants to know when Jesus will return. There's so much interest. People sit down and study and figure and calculate. But I can tell you one truth about the Second Coming; and I am sure of it. The Second Coming is nearer today than it was yesterday!

Know this: the function of faith is not to answer the question of when. It's simply to be ready. Write those words out and keep them with you: Be ready. That's what faith says to us.

Faith does answer the question of who: Jesus Christ.

When Paul wrote to Timothy, he said, "I know in whom I have believed, and I'm persuaded that he's able to keep all that I have committed unto him against that day." We read in Acts 4, that those early disciples started to spread the Christian faith like wildfire. You know how they described it? Read verse 13. These people were with Jesus.

Do you know what the heart of faith is? It's Jesus Christ. It's when we submit our lives totally and completely to him. It's when he becomes our model and our example, and we begin to trust and obey and follow. We're on the alert—we're ready because we're following after Jesus Christ.

Faith does not answer the question of why, or what, or where, or when. It does answer the question of who, and it's centered in Jesus Christ. Let me assure you, anything else you trust in can let you down. Anything else that you put your faith in can drop you in a minute. There is only one place for transformed people to put their faith, and that's in Jesus Christ. When our faith is in him, it will be totally sufficient.

FAITH DOESN'T ANSWER	FAITH DOES SAY
Why	Trust
What	Obey
Where	Follow
When	Be ready

Partnering with God

I always enjoyed playing competitive tennis. My dad told me that the most important part of playing doubles in tennis was selecting the right partner. You can win a whole lot more if you have a very good partner.

One of the great moments of my life occurred a few years ago when I was asked to participate in a large charity event in Montgomery, Alabama. I said I would accept if they would tell me what they expected me to do.

They said that the charity event had three professional tennis players coming to town for an exhibition. One of the players was Rod Laver, the only man to achieve the tennis grand slam (winning all four of tennis's major singles titles in the same year: the Australian Open, French Open, Wimbledon, and U.S. Open). Actually, Laver did it not once, but twice! They said they would like for me to be his doubles partner.

I held out the telephone receiver and shook it a little to make sure that I was hearing correctly. To have an opportunity to meet Rod Laver would be great; to play doubles with him was unbelievable! I immediately said yes.

I couldn't sleep for two or three nights before the exhibition match. Finally, the day came. Lots of people were present, and lots of money was raised. When I first met Rod Laver, I said, "It's a pleasure to meet you, Mr. Laver." He replied, "Just call me Rod." I said he could call me John Ed.

I asked if he preferred to play the forehand or backhand side of the court. He looked at me, smiled, and walked over to the alley, one of the two narrow zones on either side of the court. He said, "John Ed, if you can just cover this alley, I can take care of the rest of the court." That's the kind of partner I like to have. He was going to carry the load for us.

We won the toss, and he asked me to serve first. Since this was a charity event I thought it would be appropriate to ask everyone if they would like to bow their heads for a prayer. When the pros on the other side of the net bowed their heads, I went ahead and served. We were up 15-love before they had opened their eyes!

Having Rod Laver as a doubles partner in tennis was the best I could possibly hope for. Having Jesus Christ as my partner in life assures a victory—even in the tough times.

When transformed people team with Jesus and walk with him, we cannot help but be successful. We actually discover that even during tough times, life is meaningful and purposeful. Jesus is a faithful partner. He said, "I will never leave you or forsake you." Transformed people focus on the fundamental fact that God is always with us.

I love the old gospel song, "What a Friend We Have in Jesus." The beautiful lyrics were written by Joseph Scriven in 1855.

> What a friend we have in Jesus, all our sins and
>   griefs to bear!
> What a privilege to carry everything to God in
>   prayer!
> O what peace we often forfeit, O what needless
>   pain we bear,
> All because we do not carry everything to God in
>   prayer.
>
> Have we trials and temptations? Is there trouble
>   anywhere?
> We should never be discouraged; take it to the
>   Lord in prayer.
> Can we find a friend so faithful who will all our
>   sorrows share?
> Jesus knows our every weakness; take it to the
>   Lord in prayer.

There is another great Easter hymn, "In the Garden," written in 1912 by C. Austin Miles. The chorus says:

> And he walks with me, and he talks with me,
> And he tells me I am his own;
> And the joy we share as we tarry there,
> None other has ever known.

Transformed people stay focused on the fact that Jesus walks with us and talks with us and is the best partner we could ever have, especially during the tough times.

Take Action

These fundamentals are not offered simply as topics to be discussed, debated, analyzed, or admired. To focus on them means to commit to them and to practice them.

We are being asked to trust, obey, follow, prepare, and partner with Jesus Christ. The time for decision is not sometime in the future. The time to focus on fundamentals is now!

There's a story about a great convention of all Satan's workers. He asked them, "What is our best strategy for the twenty-first century? How can we win the world for Satan?"

One of the wise workers stood and said, "I think our best strategy is to tell people that there is no God and no Christ and no heaven and no hell and no punishment."

Satan said, "Oh, that won't work. Everything in life has consequences, so we know that strategy wouldn't work."

A second worker stood and said, "I think what we ought to do is tell people there is a God. There is a Jesus but he's not the only way, and there's a Bible but it's not completely true."

Satan said, "Oh, that'll never work. There are a lot of folks who when they read the Bible have already discovered faith in Christ, and they look up to the heavens and they see how real God is, so that won't work either."

Finally, a third worker stood and said, "I've got the perfect solution. Let's tell the world that Jesus Christ is the Son of God, and he's the only way to salvation. Let's also say that the Bible is true and that people can be saved forever. But... let's tell them not to make any decision about it now. They can put it off until another time."

Satan grinned. "That's it! If we give people an excuse to put off their decision, we'll win them for sure."

The real question is whether his strategy is working.

3.
Exercise God's Creativity

*W*hen we see birds perched on a tree limb or power line during a storm, we are tempted to think they don't know what they're doing. Although it seems illogical to humans, the birds are in fact doing just what God intended. Birds that perch have special muscles in their feet that grip the perch and hold the birds securely in place, whether they are sleeping or weathering a storm.

The world tells us that many things are impossible, and that we are not capable of completing the tasks to which we are called. The world might also tell us that working on a relationship with God isn't worth the effort.

I disagree. The Bible says that with people, some things are indeed impossible. But according to Matthew 19:27, "with God everything is possible."

Transformed people need to think outside of the box. We need to think creatively.

Finding a Way

Mark 2:1-5 provides a good example of people thinking creatively. Four men wanted to carry a lame friend to Jesus. They approached the house where Jesus was teaching and found it overflowing with people. The men knew there was no way to get through the door so that Jesus could heal their lame friend. So they dug a hole through the roof above Jesus' head, and they lowered their friend through the hole and into the house, right in front of Jesus. The Lord saw the faith of the men and healed their friend.

When the men were faced with this tough situation, the logical thing for them to say would have been: "We tried. We brought our friend to Jesus, but we couldn't get in to see him." They could have left their friend outside to fend for himself, or they could have taken him back home. But instead, these men thought creatively, and their creativity brought about the healing of their lame friend.

In tough times we can flop down like a rooster, put our wings over our head, and say we did our best; or we can think outside the box and ask for God's help in a different, creative way that exceeds our way.

Following God

Think back to the time when Joshua went to fight the battle of Jericho (Joshua 6). This is a tremendous example of how a military leader followed God's creative battle plan. God's way of doing it was so different from our way. But God found a man in Joshua who was willing to follow him, and the walls of Jericho fell.

Here is the basic principle: God's way always works. His way is right, successful, purposeful, and meaningful. And our way never works.

Another great example is found in 2 Kings 5:2-14. Even though Naaman was a valiant warrior, he was stricken with leprosy, a disease that at the time was considered hopeless. God used a little slave girl to tell Naaman about a prophet who could heal him. The prophet's name was Elisha.

When visiting Naaman, Elisha gave him the most unusual prescription that anyone could have ever heard. Elisha said Naaman should go to the Jordan River and dip himself into the water seven times. Can you imagine what people thought when they heard this? Leprosy causes open sores all over a person's body. At that time, the Jordan River was very polluted. We can imagine that the thought of stepping into the polluted waters would have been almost nauseating. Logical-thinking people would have considered Elisha's advice to be foolish.

Naaman had a choice: he could either follow God's creative way as prescribed by the prophet Elisha or continue with conventional medicine that was not working for him. He elected to go to the Jordan River.

Naaman went out into the water and dipped himself–once, twice, three times—and nothing happened. Can you imagine what onlookers were saying about him? They must have laughed and called him foolish. Six times he dipped himself and nothing happened. He might have started to walk out, and perhaps one of his officers said, "Sir, that wasn't the prescription—it was seven times." I can imagine that Naaman, though he may have been reluctant, nevertheless was obedient and dipped himself into the Jordan River for the seventh time. Naaman came out of the water, and the Bible describes his skin as being like that of a newborn baby.

God has an answer for dealing with tough times, and the answer might be totally outside the box. The real question is: Do we believe God is in charge and knows what he is doing? Then, we must decide if we are willing to follow him.

Now look at Judges 7. Gideon was ready to send his army to fight the Midianites at Moreh, but before he could go into battle, God wanted to help him select the size of his army. Gideon was concerned because he thought his army was not large enough. He had only 32,000 men. God informed him that he was partially correct. He didn't have the right number of men. His army was too large—not too small.

God told Gideon to let all the men go home who wanted to, and 22,000 accepted the invitation and went home.

This left 10,000 men. Again Gideon appealed to God, saying that he didn't have enough men to fight. God partially agreed in that Gideon did not have the right number of men. His army was still too large.

He instructed Gideon to have the men drink water. All the men who cupped their hands, dipped the water, and lifted it up to their mouths were to be in one group. The men who kneeled and lapped the water like a dog were placed in another group. Gideon realized that 9,700 men used their hands to drink the water, and only 300 lapped it like a dog.

Gideon probably approached the 9,700 thinking they must be the right group. However, God shocked Gideon by directing him to the 300. While Gideon was concerned about having too few men, God was creatively reducing the number of his men.

Gideon had a battle plan, but God had another plan. The question was, which plan would Gideon follow?

God's creative battle plan was for Gideon to take the 300 men to battle with trumpets, torches, and clay jars. Gideon thought, "What chance would 300 men armed with trumpets, torches, and clay jars have against an army more numerous than the sands of the sea?"

Although Gideon's human inclination was to scoff at reducing the number of men in his army, he elected to follow God's plan. He believed in God and trusted that God was in charge.

The basic principle is: Either we follow God and trust that he knows what he is doing, or we follow our own way of thinking and live with the consequences.

Fishing for Birds

When my son, Si, was five years old, he asked me several times to take him fishing, but we never got around to it. So for Christmas I received a present from him that was one-half-inch thick and six-feet long. Also under the Christmas tree was a small package—a jar of live worms!

Well, despite his big hint, we didn't go fishing immediately, so he decided to use his own creative genius. I came home one day and found him standing in the middle of the backyard—fishing pole, line, worms, and all. I asked him what he was doing, and he said, "Fishing for birds." I tried to explain that that wasn't the way to catch birds, but he quickly said, "Fish like worms, and you catch them on a hook. Birds like worms too, so why can't you catch them with a hook?"

I didn't have an answer to that. It sounded logical and reasonable, except that it doesn't work that way. Then I thought how often I select a way to do something that seems logical and reasonable to me, but it doesn't work out because it's not God's way. Then I thought about the Scripture verses: "There is a way that seems right to man, but the end is destruction"; "The way of a fool is right in his own eyes"; "Your ways are not my ways, says the Lord."

Investing in Faith

An important part of any economy is investments. People would never have believed how quickly investments could diminish, as they did in the second half of 2008. For many of those people, their investments were tied to retirement funds that were dramatically diminished or nonexistent. As one person said, "My 401K is now a 101K."

The problem with the world's investments is that they are not secure. There is no guarantee. While those investments will sometimes go up, they can sometimes go down, and sometimes go out of sight!

One man had a multimillion-dollar art collection in his home. His home burned, leaving nothing. Many people have invested in beautiful homes on the Gulf Coast, and hurricanes have played havoc with those investments. Sadly, many people experience the cruelty of "white collar thieves" who break into computer files and steal not only money but also a person's complete identity.

Anytime we put our investments in a worldly commodity, it is subject to thieves, moths, rust, natural disasters, and white-collar ingenuity.

Let's look at what God's economics teaches us about investments. In Matthew 6:19-20, Jesus said, "Do not lay up for yourselves treasures upon earth where moths and rust destroy and where thieves break in and steal, but lay up for yourselves treasures in heaven, where neither moths or rust destroys nor thieves break in or steal."

God's economics deals with this life and for eternity. If we lay up our treasures in heaven, we have invested our time and energy and resources wisely. He also says that there will be many rewards in heaven.

The problem with earthly investments is that they end when our heart beats the last time. I have never officiated at a funeral where a person hooked up a U-Haul to carry along some of their investments into the hereafter.

God's economic system is entirely different from the world's. If our investments are in heaven, we get to enjoy them forever and ever and ever and ever. In Luke 12:33, Jesus indicates that the best investment is giving. He says you can then have a purse that does not wear out. He refers to it as unfailing treasure in heaven where no thief or moth or anything else can get to it.

The investments in God's economics haven't failed in thousands of years, and will be here for all eternity. God is the only one offering a no-risk, high-yield investment. Transformed people make wise choices when investing in faith.

God's Collateral

Businesses that function well during tough times are willing to do things differently and creatively. Similarly, successful people are usually able to think outside the box.

A rumpled man walks into a bank in New York City and asks for the loan officer. He says he is going to Europe on business for two weeks and needs to borrow $5,000.

The bank officer says the bank will need some kind of security for such a loan. So the man—clearly an eccentric—hands over the keys to a new Rolls Royce parked in front of the bank. Everything checks out, and the bank agrees to accept the car as collateral for the loan. An employee drives the Rolls into the bank's underground garage and parks it there.

Two weeks later the man returns and repays the $5,000, along with interest that came to $15.41. The loan officer says, "We are very happy to have had your business, and this transaction has worked out very nicely, but we are a little puzzled. While you were away, we checked you out and found that you are a multimillionaire. Why would you bother to borrow $5,000?"

The man replies, "Where else in New York can I park my car for two weeks and pay fifteen bucks?"

One of the important ingredients in economics is an understanding of collateral. The world has one view; God's economics offers quite a different perspective.

Early in the twenty-first century, the world's economics got into trouble because collateral was taken lightly. We saw what happened when money was lent to people who did not have proper collateral. Subprime loans, mortgage lending, and questionable financing helped cause the bottom to drop out of the United States's economy and affected many other nations throughout the world.

God's economics teaches us that with God you don't have to put up any physical possessions as collateral. All God requires is for us to trust in him and commit to "do as I say."

Read Matthew 21:28-31. In this passage, Jesus told a parable about a man who had two sons. The man asked both sons to go to work in his business. One of them said: "Sure, Dad, I would be glad to go to work. I look forward to working in your business." But he decided not to go to work. The second one had a different attitude. He said, "Dad, I don't care about working for you today," but later he changed his mind and went to work.

Jesus then challenged the crowd by asking the question, "Which of those sons did what his father expected—the one who said he would do it but did not, or the one who at first declined but then followed through and performed?"

In God's economics, collateral is commitment with integrity. It is obedience. It is not just talking, but walking.

Malachi made this clear when he raised a question about robbing God (Malachi 3). The people of Israel insisted they had not robbed God. Malachi disagreed, saying that the people's command had been to bring the tithe into the storehouse, and they had not done this. God, through Malachi, even invited the nation to test his economic policy.

As always, God offered a second chance. Through Malachi, God invited the people to do what he told them, then promised that he would open up the windows of heaven and pour out blessings such as they had never known. That is God's economics!

In 1839, John D. Rockefeller was born in New York, and as a teenager he moved with his family to Cleveland, Ohio. He became interested in crude oil production, and in 1870 he formed the Standard Oil Company.

Rockefeller became the biggest producer of crude oil in the United States, then ventured out into other enterprises. By the time he retired in 1911, Rockefeller was worth $1 billion.

When asked about his secret of success, Rockefeller said, "When I was a child I was taught that everything I had was a gift from God. God gave me talent in order to use it, but it is to be returned to him, so I started returning ten percent of everything that he allowed me to make. I have always done that."

Many people were surprised to discover that more than half of what Rockefeller earned, he gave away. Someone commented, "It is easy to tithe if you have a billion dollars." Rockefeller responded, "I started out making $1.50 a week. The first $1.50 I got, I gave a tenth to my church. If I had not started tithing on $1.50 a week, I would not have been able to tithe on a billion dollars today."

Understanding collateral is essential to understanding God's economics. For God, collateral is not anything tangible that you offer—it is a commitment to be faithful and obedient.

God's view of collateral has worked for thousands of years and will continue to work forever. Questionable financing will always have a hole in it and will never substitute for commitment and integrity.

The story of man's relationship to God is the story of how God is always thinking creatively and trying to get us to follow him. One of the crucial things about living in tough times is whether or not we are willing to do things God's way.

Everlasting Arms

I recently had the privilege of preaching at the annual Hartselle Camp Meeting in Hartselle, Alabama. This camp meeting began in 1899 and has been held every year since. The worship services are still held in the tabernacle that was built that first year. The supports for the tabernacle are made from large cypress trees that once grew on the property.

Among the first musicians to lead the music there was Anthony J. Showalter. At the time, he had friends who had experienced the loss of loved ones. With their burden on his heart, Showalter went to the tabernacle and wrote down his thoughts. Those thoughts were an expression of the tough times his friends were facing, and his answer to facing them. Those inspired thoughts became the refrain of the great hymn, "Leaning on the Everlasting Arms." (Later, Showalter's associate Elisha Hoffman contributed the verses for the hymn.)

Showalter's friends were facing tough times, and he knew on whom his friends needed to lean in order to find stability and security. What a comfort these words continue to bring:

What a fellowship, what a joy divine,
  leaning on the everlasting arms;
What a blessedness, what a peace is mine,
  leaning on the everlasting arms.

What have I to dread, what have I to fear, leaning on the ever
  lasting arms;
I have blessed peace with my Lord so near, leaning on the everlasting arms.

Leaning, leaning, safe and secure from all alarms;
Leaning, leaning, leaning on the everlasting arms.

George Beverly Shea, longtime soloist for the Billy Graham Crusade, knew how this hymn came about, and for many years he had wanted to visit Hartselle to see the tabernacle where the hymn got its start. In 2007, at age ninety-seven, Shea asked my friend Phil Waldrep to take him and his wife to the tabernacle. As Shea stood where Showalter had stood 120 years earlier, he sang from memory the entire hymn. Phil said it was one of the greatest spiritual moments of his life.

Shea, too, had experienced some really tough times in his life. He had discovered the same answer to dealing with those problems as had Anthony Showalter. Their discovery can be our experience today.

I was able to stand in the same tabernacle, in the same place, as those two great musicians. I didn't try to sing the hymn, but I did quote it, and it drove home to me even more the fact that we can rise above the storms of life. I felt that I joined a heavenly chorus of transformed people who knew on whom to lean in order to navigate the tough times.

Ultimate success in dealing with tough times is dependent not on our education or expertise or training; it is ultimately based on our willingness to follow God's creative plan for each situation.

4.
Develop a Christlike Attitude

*I*f a bird is ready for migration or wanting to find a better
food source, it can use a storm to its benefit. It can position
itself ahead of the wind and use the swift storm currents to
propel it to a new location. The bird is able to see possibilities, not
problems, in the face of the storm.

In my life I have discovered that attitude is more important
than the reality of situations. I've seen people who were facing similar situations emerge with opposite results because of
their attitudes. We have little or no control over the situation
itself, but we can and must be in control of our attitude. In my
opinion, attitude determines the outcome of most situations.

Paul reminds us in Philippians 2:5, "Your attitude should be
the same as that of Christ Jesus" (NIV).The attitude that will help
us transcend tough times is the attitude that Jesus had.

Drinking from the Cup

In 2009, an outbreak of flu caused by the H1N1 virus caused
people to take a variety of measures to keep the virus from

spreading. In the area where I live, high school athletic events were cancelled, businesses and churches handed out instructions about how to avoid catching and passing on the flu, and other preventative measures were taken.

We try to stop the spread of disease, but it occurred to me that there are some things for which we need to encourage an epidemic. We need to see some things spread rapidly.

I would like to see a contagious outbreak of Christian commitment, Christian witness, church attendance, prayer, Bible study, and more. These would be excellent epidemics!

Ask yourself: Is there something about me that people ought to catch? What would happen to the gross domestic product in the United States if everybody caught my work ethic? What would people's trust level be if everybody caught my core ethical values? What kind of atmosphere would pervade our country if everybody caught my attitude?

There is one thing that I hope we can all catch. I learned it from a man I admire and with whom I serve on the Board of The United Methodist Publishing House. Dr. Robert Spain is a retired United Methodist Bishop and serves as chaplain to the Publishing House.

Bob tells about his first pastorate at a small church in rural Shawnatee, Tennessee. The leader of that church was William Dixon, known affectionately as Uncle Billy. Uncle Billy was quite elderly. He had one eye, and he had lost one arm. He was the patriarch of the community, and everybody loved him.

Even though the church had elected officials, Uncle Billy was the one who really made the decisions. Before the worship service every Sunday morning, he made the announcements. When he was ready to make the announcements, he would simply tuck the paperback hymnal under his arm, walk up, and start talking. Bob said, "I learned to just sit down and let him say what he had to say."

About that time, a mysterious illness began to spread among the people in Shawnatee. People became seriously ill. A public health nurse came in from Knoxville to investigate.

The nurse determined that the illness was due to the fact that people were all drinking from the same dipper that hung on a well located between the school and town. Anyone who was thirsty would simply drop the bucket in the well, pull it up, and use the dipper to get a drink of water. After discovering the cause, the nurse came to Bob and asked for his help to inform the people and stop this practice.

Now, Bob knew that in small rural towns, people don't take kindly to big-city folks telling them what to do. So he asked Uncle Billy to tell the people in the church and help spread the word. Uncle Billy agreed to tell them the following Sunday morning.

At the worship service, Uncle Billy pleaded with the congregation to stop drinking from that dipper. They listened and they would obey—no doubt about it.

Uncle Billy then tucked his paperback hymnal under his arm and knelt at the communion table. Removing a white cloth from the communion elements, he lifted the cover off a communion tray and took out one of the little cups. Holding the cup, he walked back and forth in front of the first row, spilling some of the grape juice as he did. Then, with intense emotion, Uncle Billy exclaimed, "Let's all drink from this cup and catch what Jesus had!"

Uncle Billy was right. We need to catch what Jesus had. We need to spread it. Let's start an epidemic!

When we face a tough situation, we have one of two choices: we can see the situation as a problem or as a possibility. The normal human attitude focuses on problems. The Christlike attitude focuses on possibilities.

Problems or Possibilities

In John 6, we read that a crowd of over 5,000 people listened to Jesus teach. Because the crowd had been there so long, they were getting hungry. The disciples came to Jesus, worried about how to feed that many people.

Phillip stated that even if food was available, they wouldn't have enough money to buy it. He said they could work for months and not earn enough to feed the crowd.

Phillip and the disciples' attitude led them to see a problem. Jesus' attitude presented a possibility.

Jesus asked his listeners whether there was any food available and was told that one young boy had five barley loaves and two fish. Taking the loaves and fish, Jesus blessed them and gave them to the people. After everyone had eaten plenty, the disciples collected the leftovers—twelve baskets full!

When the disciples saw a problem, Jesus saw a possibility. This story assures us that Jesus is bigger than any situation. He can handle any problem. If we give him what we have, he can take it and multiply it. A little becomes a lot when placed in God's hands.

In 1914, Thomas Edison lost thirteen buildings at his phonograph factory. Fire had broken out in the film room, where highly flammable materials caught fire. As a result, six buildings burned to the ground, and seven suffered extensive damage.

What would have been devastation for most people served as motivation for Edison. He declared that the factory would resume manufacturing within ten days, and then set about to improve the factory design.

Edison told his son, "We've just cleared out a bunch of old rubbish! We'll build bigger and better on these ruins."

In Edison's way of thinking, all the ideas that didn't work were gone. Now he could focus on the ideas that did work. His most productive years followed that fire. He saw the fire not as a problem but a possibility.

Serving or Being Served

The mother of James and John went to Jesus to ask for a favor. She requested that her two sons sit at a place of honor, at the right and left of Jesus.

Jesus told her that what she was asking would be difficult to grant. Even though she was convinced that her sons were deserving, Jesus had a different attitude. He told her that it was not his prerogative to assign those seats, but rather his father's choice.

When the other disciples heard about this, they were critical of James and John. Jesus saw this as an opportunity to teach them about a new attitude. Jesus said, "Whoever wants to be a leader among you must be your servant, and whoever wants to be first among you must become your slave. For even the Son of Man came not to be served but to serve others and to give his life as a ransom for many" (Matthew 20:28 NLT).

The attitude of the disciples was to see how they could be rewarded. They felt that being a disciple had its perks. They were eager to cash in on their membership privileges. Jesus quickly informed them that his membership privileges meant that they could be last and that they could serve.

The disciples weren't the only ones who were confused about this concept. In church, some people want to know about the perks of membership. They ask: "Does it mean we get preferential treatment?" "Does it mean we can park close to the building?" "Does it mean we can have a reserved seat in the sanctuary?"

A Christlike attitude really means the opposite: We gladly give up our seats to first-time visitors. We park at the back of the parking lot and save places closest to the door for visitors or people with special needs. We serve through the church rather than look for ways the church can serve us. We do not ask what the church can do for us; we ask what we can do for Jesus Christ as we serve in his church.

On the last night he lived, Jesus gathered his disciples in an upper room to have a final meal with them. Before eating, he took a towel and basin, knelt down, and began to wash his disciples' feet. This was one of the lowest acts a person could perform; not even a slave was required to wash his master's feet.

When Peter protested, Jesus told him, "Unless I wash you, you won't belong to me." So Peter said, "Then wash my hands and head as well, Lord, not just my feet!" After Jesus had washed the disciples' feet, he wanted to make sure they understood his attitude and followed his example. He said, "I tell you the truth, slaves are not greater than their master. Nor is the messenger more important than the one who sends the message. Now that you know these things, God will bless you for doing them" (John 13:1-17 NLT).

The last night that Jesus lived, he was betrayed by Judas and arrested by Roman soldiers. One disciple used a sword to cut off the ear of a soldier, but Jesus stopped him. The attitude of the disciples was to respond with weapons and force, but the attitude of Jesus was to offer a life of love and sacrifice. What sounded foolish to Jesus' followers, he used to bring the ultimate victory.

Serving Effectively

The attitude of Jesus was not to just say something, but to do it. The best way to face tough times is not only to know what Jesus said, but to follow his example.

I have had many people tell me their stories following a natural disaster. Some people cave in because they lost so much in a hurricane—others lament the fact that their possessions were lost, but decide to go in another direction and become even more successful.

Tough times might bring us to our knees, humble us, and allow us to look for creative ways that we might serve more effectively. Sometimes tough times help the church see opportunities for service. When hurricanes hit the Gulf Coast region during recent years, our church was able to open up the facilities and become a shelter for hundreds of people. While it was a very tragic situation, I have had some people say that the hurricane and the tough times that followed changed their whole attitude toward church because they found a church that reached out to them and cared for them.

The question is: How might we serve more effectively? Tough economic times often give the church an opportunity to develop ministries to train people for employment, and to help them find jobs. Some churches start food pantries, clothes closets, and other creative ministries to people in need.

Transformed people discover that tough times can result in multiple ways to serve.

Developing a Relationship with God

The attitude of Jesus was not just to be busy and productive but also to spend time with his father. Sometimes tough times give us more of an opportunity to develop our relationship with God.

One day Jesus stopped at the home of Mary and Martha while on his way to Jerusalem. The women welcomed him into their home. Martha focused on preparing a large meal for Jesus and the disciples, while her sister Mary sat down and listened to Jesus. Martha became exasperated with Mary and asked Jesus to have Mary come and help in the kitchen. But Jesus had a different perspective.

He said, "My dear Martha, you are worried and upset over all these details! There is only one thing worth being concerned about. Mary has discovered it, and it will not be taken away from her" (Luke 10:38-42 NLT).

Martha did not understand the importance of spending time with Jesus. The attitude of Jesus was to spend time alone with his father. He would often leave a crowd and spend time talking with God. When transformed people spend time with God, they discover the necessity of developing a relationship with him.

Trusting God

We can't change the circumstances of life very often, but we can change our attitude. Most of us will not have much influence on the stock market or the economy or global politics or how many hurricanes will come this season. We are not in control of these things, but we must be in control of our attitude toward them. Our attitude toward a situation is more important than the problem.

Physical illness can produce tough times. We tend to think that people should live forever. We always want to pray for complete healing. I believe in healing, but sometimes perfect healing comes when a transformed person enters into heaven where there is no more crying or pain, no more illness. The plan of Jesus was not for people to live forever. Sometimes death is not a defeat but the ultimate victory and perfect healing.

In life, most situations are neither good nor bad in themselves. It depends on what we let God make of the situation. The inherent value of the situation is determined by the degree to which we allow God to use it.

A dictionary has a lot of words in it. That's neither good nor bad. A lewd, terrible mind can take words from that dictionary and write pornographic, ugly, evil things that tear people down. Another person can use words from the same dictionary and write a great hymn of praise or a letter of encouragement. It's what you do with what is there.

When you go to a doctor, the doctor might write a prescription for you. That prescription is neither good nor bad—it depends on what you do with it. If you just ignore the prescription, it'll do you no good. If you take it as the doctor has prescribed for you, it will help you get well. If you abuse that prescription, it can be the worst thing that ever happened to you.

I've met some athletes who let their talents go to their heads, and they became arrogant people whom nobody wanted to be around. Other athletes committed their talents to God and let him use their talent as a platform for ministry.

Shaun Alexander was a great running back for the University of Alabama. He went on to establish rushing records in the

National Football League and be named Most Valuable Player in the league. Speaking at Frazer United Methodist Church, he said, "God gave me my talent, and I want to develop my talent to be the best football player I can be for the purpose of allowing God to use me to be a witness for him." That is a Christlike attitude toward life!

Tough times will come—often at unexpected times. They make us bitter or better. They make us or break us. We can either react to them as eagles or as roosters. Our choices determine the outcome.

This book has sought to identify some ways to gauge tough times and learn to handle them effectively. Be open to other ways in which God can help you rise above the storm.

Dear brothers and sisters, when troubles come your way, consider it an opportunity for great joy. For you know that when your faith is tested, your endurance has a chance to grow. So let it grow, for when your endurance is fully developed, you will be perfect and complete, needing nothing.

James 1:2-4 NLT

For Reflection and Discussion

1. Return to Priorities

Read and discuss Psalm 23.

1. Why do you think sheep feel secure with their shepherd?

2. Is it possible to be too successful? How can success create tough times?

3. What is meant by the following statement? "It is difficult to hold a full cup with a steady hand, especially if that cup was filled quickly."

4. Are there ways in which you have drifted away from your priorities because of lack of focus? What has been the result?

5. What steps can you take to rediscover and realign your priorities?

6. How are your priorities demonstrated by the way you spend your time? your money? Give examples.

7. Describe some times in your life when you made choices based on your feelings. What happened?

8. Describe some times in your life when you made choices based on God's direction. What happened?

2. Focus on Fundamentals

Read and discuss Matthew 14:22–33.

1. Recall a time when you were paralyzed by fear. How can transformed people turn fear into faith?

2. Why are fundamentals important to success in sports and other activities? Name some examples you've seen or experienced.

3. What is meant by the following statement? "If you swallow the fear, it will poison you."

4. Discuss some differences between financial security and God's security.

5. Have there been situations in your life when you have focused on the circumstances rather than on Jesus Christ? What was the result?

6. What are some examples of tough times that you have faced? How did you respond to them?

7. Think of times when you put your faith in people or things, rather than only in God. What difference did you experience between the two approaches?

8. Have there been times when you were not sure where you were going in your life? Describe them. What was your response?

3. Exercise God's Creativity

Read and discuss Judges 7.

1. What have you done that the world said was impossible? How did God's creativity turn that impossible task into a possible success?

2. What is meant by the following statement? "Transformed people need to think outside the box."

3. What do Joshua, Naaman, and Gideon have in common?

4. How are God's economics different from human economics?

5. How are your listening skills with people? With God? When you have listened to God, what has he told you?

6. Are you trusting and honest with yourself? Describe some ways in which you are and aren't.

7. Have you experienced times when you didn't see God or understand his will? If so, what did you do?

8. Describe a situation you have experienced when you chose to respond in the same way you have always responded. Describe a situation when you responded in a new, creative way.

4. Develop a Christlike Attitude

Read and discuss Luke 10:38-42.

1. Describe a time when you saw a problem but God showed you that it was really an opportunity.

2. How do you think a Christlike attitude can affect your life during tough times?

3. Discuss some ways in which epidemics affect individuals and communities.

4. What did Uncle Billy mean by his statement? "Let's all drink from this cup and catch what Jesus had!"

5. How did Thomas Edison view the fire at his factory? What are some other examples of a problem becoming a possibility?

6. Name some areas of your daily life in which you could benefit from a Christ-like attitude. What are some things you could do to achieve it?

7. Evaluate some of the ways in which you serve. What are some things you could do to serve more effectively?

8. What do you do each day that helps you develop a relationship with God? What can you do to deepen this relationship?